Bob Brooks has a long association with practical gardening going back to his school days in the mid-thirties when he helped his father in his market garden plot in the Fortwilliam district of his native Belfast. His service in the RAF during the World War 2 and in the post war years took him to India, Burma, Africa and Germany.

He took up gardening as a leisure activity when he completed his RAF service in 1953.

Bob made a special study of growing techniques and over the years he acquired considerable expertise in the cultivation of roses, clematis and many other plants.

Now in retirement he is in great demand as a speaker on all aspects of gardening and travels extensively throughout Ireland giving talks to a variety of interested groups.

His own showpiece garden in Eastleigh Drive, Belfast is a mecca for gardening enthusiasts and is much visited throughout the summer, often by overseas visitors. At times the garden resembles a doctor's surgery when callers bring along their ailing plants for a diagnosis and advice on treatment.

An acknowledged authority on rose growing and the cultivation of fuchsias and clematis Bob is president of the Irish Fuchsia Society and area representative for both the Royal National Rose Society and the British Clematis Society. He is a Fellow of the Rose Society of Northern Ireland.

— · —— · —— · —— · —— · ——

Mahonia aquifolium (Oregon grape)

This is an evergreen low-growing shrub with attractive foliage which turns red in winter. Fragrant bunches of small yellow flowers appear in Spring followed by blue-black berries.

As we enter the new year we will see a glorious display of colour from the winter flowering bulbs if the weather is reasonably mild.

The crocus family is always dependable for its carpet of colour and the popular snowdrops (galanthus), the winter aconites (eranthis) and colourful cyclamen varieties.

Shrubs

We will also welcome a delightful variety of fragrance and colour from the early flowering shrubs. The wintersweet (Chimonanthus), the honeysuckle (Lonicera fragrantissima), Hamamelis mollis, Daphne Mezereum, Viburnum farreri and the lovely Mahonia family.

These shrubs are worthy of a place in every garden and they can be relied upon year after year to provide fragrance and colour in those cold days of mid-winter.

Seed Sowing

It is now time to get seeds started into growth if there is a heated greenhouse or a propagator. Plants for bedding later on and for baskets and other containers will benefit from early sowing. They will be well on by spring and robust plants by planting out time.

The half-hardies needing heat for germination are: Antirrhinums, fibrous begonias, carnations, gloxinias, lobelia, phlox and French and African marigolds.

Sweet peas are best sown much earlier for strong plants. It is not too late to get them into propagation now for large plants ready for planting out in May. Plant 10 - 15 seeds evenly spaced in a 15cm (6in.) pot of good potting compost. Pinch out the tips of the plants at 20cm (8in.) and plant out in a single clump without root disturbance in fertile to rich soil in a sunny position in May for a glorious display of colour in summer. It will pay to liquid feed weekly.

New Plants for the Garden.

This is a good time to make those changes which you may have noted during the past growing season.

It is good practice to take notes throughout the seasons recording desirable changes.

Crocus and snowdrops

Viburnum Tinus
Eva Price

This is an attractive and long flowering variety and it is evergreen.

The aspect of the garden in relation to the sun should be noted when planning a planting scheme. Most plants prefer an open sunny and sheltered position. The south and West of the garden will get the most sun. If the garden is shady it will be necessary to think specifically of plants which prefer shaded situations.

Good preparation of the soil is essential. It is important to include plenty of well rotted manure or garden compost and a liberal portion of bone meal or a fish, blood and bone meal mix. A soil that has been well prepared will ensure that the plants will romp away by early spring,

Remember. the South and West of the garden will get the most sun.

Skimmia reevesiana

Crocus augustifolius, spring flowering

This is the latest addition to the Skimmia family. Superb flowers and berries. A hermaphrodite (self-pollinating) variety.

Heathers can be relied on for a good display all year round and they are always colourful even when not in flower. A sunny position suits them best.

ight levels will begin to improve this month as the days lengthen and, provided outdoor temperatures rise a little, we will see new growth on trees and the shrubs. The rising sap is a sure sign that spring is not far away.

Preparation for sowing outdoors in early spring should continue. Clear away weeds which may have reappeared since last month and have a general clean sweep of all garden debris.

Cloches should be positioned now so that the soil is warm and ready for sowing seeds where an early crop is desired.

There is still time to sow seeds for summer bedding plants in a heated greenhouse or propagator.

Dahlia tubers can be started into growth this month. Any tubers found to be shrivelled can be steeped in tepid water overnight to make them plump and ready for producing new flowering shoots. Maximum light is necessary to help the tubers to sprout.

Kalmia latifolia

Chrysanth Cuttings

Indoor chrysanths should also be started into growth now and young cuttings taken when the shoots are 7.5cm (3in) long. Cut them cleanly at the base, remove the two lower leaves and trim them just a little below the node i.e.. where the lower leaves join the stem.

Dip the cuttings into hormone rooting powder. Plant them 5cm (2in) deep around the rim of a pot of mixed potting compost and course sand (50/50). The cuttings will root quite quickly if they are placed into a heated propagator.

Mid-February is the time for pruning your late flowering clematis including the popular C.Jackmanii.

Cut them hard back to 45cm(18ins) above ground level. These varieties flower on the new wood produced in the current year and it is therefore necessary to remove most of last year's growth which will not flower again.

Syringa (Lilac).

The Spring flowering clematis, including the very popular Alpinas, Macropetalas and the Montanas, do not require regular annual pruning. If they have outgrown their allotted space they should be pruned back a little as soon as they have finished flowering - i.e.towards the end of May/ early June.

The large flowered hybrid clematis which flower in early June need only a little pruning now. Thin out weak shoots and cut back last year's growth just a little (no more than 20 cm (8in). The popular Nelly Moser is in this group.

Shrubs

There is only a little time left to plant out bare root shrubs. The hedging plants - privet, beech, hornbeam, hawthorn and the bedding roses should be planted out before the end of the month if the ground is not frozen. Good soil preparation is essential. Deep digging and adding plenty of well rotted manure or compost and a good handful of base fertiliser to the root area of the plants will ensure maximum growth.

A surface dressing of a granular fertiliser, when planting has been completed, is well worthwhile.

Leucothoe

Aucuba variegatum

A fine display of daffodils at Grovelands, Belfast.

Hedera helix angularius aurea

This excellent ivy needs good light to keep the foliage in good colour.

S pring is the busiest time of the year for the gardener. We must now finalise our tree and shrub planting programme.

Plants bought in containers from your garden centre can be planted out at any time of the year provided the soil is not frozen.

Bare rooted trees and shrubs should have been planted by late February. If they have not yet been planted this task should be completed without further delay.

Spring planting ensures that the plants are reasonably well established before winter arrives.

Clematis in liners can be planted out now into the open ground. Good soil preparation is essential. Incorporate a good liberal portion of well rotted manure or compost and a heavy handful of bone meal or fish, blood and bone fertiliser.

Roses in liners should also be planted into their permanent positions now. A fertile to rich soil suits them best. Provide a sunny spot, out of shade and sheltered from strong winds.

Dividing Perennials

Herbaceous perennials which have developed a large root system can be lifted and divided now.

The Shasta daisy (Leucanthemum), anthemis, Hardy Geranium, Hostas and Hucheras etc. are all easy to propagate by root division. Lift them and break or chop off with a spade portions of the plant with plenty of root attached. Take the portions from around the outer edge of the plant and discard the centre portion.

A good sized plant should produce at least six portions (divisions) for replanting. Enrich the new planting areas well with manure or compost and a base fertiliser for a superb show of flowers in summer.

Mid-March is a good time to prune bedding roses. The large flowered hybrids (Hybrid teas) and the clusterflowered types (floribundas) should be pruned back to about 20cm (8in) if this is their first year. Older established roses respond to a reduction of about half their previous seasons growth. A liberal feed of a suitable granular fertiliser will ensure a good supply of blooms throughout the summer.

A good time for pruning bedding roses

Elaeagnus Macrophylla

The Lawn

Pay attention to the lawn and if moss was a problem last year and was not attended to last autumn - take effective action now.

The principal causes of moss on the lawn are poor drainage, very acid soil, heavy shaded areas and poor soil fertility.

It is important to have a regular grass maintenance programme to keep your grass in peak condition. Good feeding will go a long way towards improving the grass and in some cases moss can be eliminated by giving grass greater vigour through feeding. Feed with a good quality fertiliser in early April and again in July.

Seed sowing

There is still time to sow Sweet peas if they were not sown in pots last November in the greenhouse. Seeds can be sown directly into the ground now where they are to flower or, if you have pot grown seedlings ready in the greenhouse, they can be hardened off now before planting out. Leave them outside during the day and return them to the greenhouse at night. They will harden off in a few weeks.

Try growing Sweetpeas in a large container. A 40cm (16in) pot is ideal. Make sure that it has drainage holes and fill with good quality peat based compost and John Innes soil based compost No3 -50/50 mix.

Place 3 X 2m (61/2 ft.) long canes at equal distances around the pot (120 degrees) to form a wigwam and tie the canes together at the top.

Sow about a dozen seeds from the centre to the outer edge of the pot or plant into the pot a pot of seedlings from the greenhouse if these were sown earlier.

The plants will quickly climb up the canes to the top of the wigwam. Liquid feed weekly for a glorious display of flowers and remove the spent flowers as soon as they appear.

A room with a view
Pot culture is an added attraction in the garden area.

Abutilon vitafolium

This shrub has very attractive blue flowers in early summer. Give the plant a sheltered position in good light·

Springtime in the Garden

W e are now well into Spring and plant growth will be quite rapid. The rain and warmer weather also encourages weed growth with annual weeds well to the fore.

Remove the worst intruders, chickweed and bitter cress, before they flower and this will prevent proliferation from their seed next year. The perennial weeds may need a herbicide (Glyphosate) to kill them off.

Hardy annual seed and vegetables can be sown now if weather conditions are favourable. The ground should be well prepared by removing weeds and plant debris. A good friable surface area where the soil is fine and free of stones is necessary.
Raking and treading will give an excellent firm surface for sowing. The area should be free from shade, have good light, sheltered from cold winds and the soil fertile.

Plant Feeding

Now is the time to feed shrubs to get them off to a good start for a grand summer display. A good handful of granular fertiliser spread on the soil surface will work wonders. Roses, Hydrangeas, Buddleias, and fruit trees are particularly responsive to such treatment. Roses and Hydrangeas are very hungry plants and will give a superb show of flowers if they are given a second feed in mid-June.
Liquid feeding and foliar feeding are highly recommended for sustained growth throughout the growing season.
Garden pests will soon be showing signs of their presence. Prevent leaf and flower damage now by taking the appropriate precautions. Organic sprays and slug traps are available in your garden centre.

Seed Sowing.

Seeds with a hard outer coat can be quite slow to break (germinate). Steep them in luke-warm water for a few hours or slightly chip a little off the coat to reveal the flesh. This allows the seed to germinate quite quickly.

Pieris forrestii

A most colourful ornamental shrub. It does best in semi-shade and in peaty acid soil. The flowers are superb when the plant matures.

Parsley can take up to 8 weeks to germinate.
For quick germination sow the seeds in shallow drills in well prepared fertile soil and firm the surface.
Pour boiling water over the seed surface area and you will see the parsley coming through the soil in a week or ten days.

For other seeds which are slow to break such as parsnips - place newspaper strips one inch wide on moist towelling and place the large seeds singly on the paper one inch apart. Keep the towelling moist and in a short time you will see the seeds sprout.
Cut strips of the paper one inch long with a seed on each piece and plant out (cover with soil).
Your parsnips will quickly form upper growth for cropping in 10 to 12 weeks.

The greenhouse is a valuable addition to the garden.

Choisya Ternata Sundance

The golden Mexican orange blossom is an excellent choice for a sheltered aspect in full sun. Provide a fertile acid soil for best results.

Embothrium Longifolium

Clematis montana rubens

Pictured in Bob's garden, this very vigorous pink variety will, with support, eventually reach up to 10m (30ft).

Preparing for Summer

This month sees lots of new growth and flowers on fruit trees, the flowering cherries, forsythias, lilacs, the azaleas and rhododendrons. We will see clear evidence of approaching summer by the end of the month and we will be able to spend a longer time in the garden in the evenings.

There are lots of pleasant jobs to do in preparation for summer.

Containers and hanging baskets can now be planted up ready for hardening off for planting out in early June. Do not be tempted to plant them out too early. A short sharp frost can appear up to late May. A regular liquid feed will provide lots of flowers throughout summer and most of autumn.

Take time to harden off half-hardy bedding plants and the fuchsias and pelargoniums. These plants thrive outside provided it is not too cold. If there is a chance of frost return the plants to the greenhouse or other sheltered area.

Plant out Dahlias, Chrysanths and Lillies mid to late May if weather conditions are favourable. There is still plenty of time to sow hardy and half hardy annuals for flowering later in the summer.

Still plenty of time to sow hardy and half-hardy annuals for late summer.

Roses

Start to spray with a fungicide and an insecticide now and remove suckers if they have appeared i.e. growths appearing from below the grafting union. Keep the rose bed free of weeds.

Regular foliar feeding now with a liquid fertiliser will pay dividends later on in the season.

Vegetables

Seeds can be sown now for a succession of crops. Lettuce, peas, carrots, beetroot and courgettes etc. Avoid gluts, specially with lettuce which are fast growing. A fortnightly sowing will ensure a continuous supply throughout summer with no losses due to bolting.

Fix supports for climbing French beans and runner beans and sow or plant them out by the end of the month.

Keep ahead of weeds. A little time spent every day on this task will not be irksome and will go a long way towards keeping the growing areas clear.

Rhododendrons are at their best this month.

Late May is a good time to remove spent flowers from trees and shrubs. This will divert the plants energy to the production of new flowering wood for next year rather than producing unwanted seeds. Rhododendrons, Azaleas, Camellias and Pieris benefit greatly when spent flowers are removed after flowering has finished.

Prevent leaves, twigs and other debris from entering a water butt by using a filter. Put a section of old tights over the end of the downpipe and secure with a rubber band. Clear out the filter regularly, especially after heavy rain.

Ceanothus with Buddleia globusa

Azaleas are the small leaved and usually small flowered rhododendrons and they are ideal for the small garden.

Crinodendron Tricuspaderia

William Morris

This Austin rose is a really good grower with a rich fruity fragrance.

The long awaited summer has arrived and the preparations for a glorious display of colour in the garden should now be finalised.

There is still time to fill all those vacant spaces in the borders with plants. In addition to all the wonderful colourful shrubs available in the garden centres there is also a very wide choice of bedding plants in plugs and in sections giving instant colour soon after planting. These bedders are also ideal for filling containers including hanging baskets and for 'dot' planting.

Display containers

Use containers for mass planting. They come in a wide variety of shapes and sizes and at moderate cost. When planted up with colourfulful annuals and Fuchsias, Pelargoniums, Begonias etc. they can be stationed at various places outside the house, on the patio and at those dull places where they can transform the area giving a warm display of colour.

Hanging Baskets

There are lots of trailing plants for all situation and these are particularly good in hanging baskets.

Large glazed pots are also available in a great variety of distinctive colours and they are particularly suited to permanent planting for Camelias,Ives, Hebes, Choisyas Pieris etc. They look really good when pot colour and plant colour contrast e.g.- a bright yellow foliage choisya ternata Sundance in a deep blue glazed pot is quite stunning. If this arrangement is edged with light cream/yellow ivies the display is even better and it is colourful all year through.

Hanging baskets are an essential added attraction for displaying colour around the outside of the house. They look their best when well filled and suspended so that the basket is at eye level. It is a mistake to set them too high. Ideally they should be viewed so that the entire basket can be seen - not just the lower part.

Regular liquid feeding will provide a long summer of colour for all your containers including the hanging baskets.

Sunseeker - a vigorous patio rose.

Lincoln Star -This summer-flowering clematis is a good choice for pot culture, deep pink flowers with red anthers all summer long.

Fuchsias

Fuchsias will make rapid growth this month. They grow much better when planted outside and out of direct sun. Pinch out the growing tips at least once to encourage the plants to produce side shoots and more flowers.
Keep the plants fed and do not let them dry out.

Lawn care

A June application of a high nitrogen grass fertiliser will produce a lush lawn for the rest of the summer and into Autumn. Feeding with the special lawn fertiliser will suppress lawn weeds and will get the grass growing really well.
The more frequently the grass is cut the better - twice weekly is ideal. Close cutting is not recommended for domestic lawns. Delay cutting during periods of drought or raise the blades.

Dead Heading

Dead-head roses regularly and when a flower head has finished prune it back a little to a lower set of leaves to encourage repeat flowering. Keep up the spraying programme with a fungicide and an insecticide spray.
Roses should be given their second granular feed by mid-June. A good handful of rose fertiliser is required for each plant and this to be spread onto the root area and tickled in with a hand fork. Keep the fertiliser off stems and foliage.

Dictamnus, the burning bush

Mixed rose bushes

Mme Julia Correvon & Jackmanii Superba - They flower at the same time and they have a good combination of colour.

A very fine display of colour is available from hardy and half hardy annuals throughout summer and into early autumn.

Time to Relax

High summer in the garden is the highlight of the year for the keen gardener. We should now see the garden at its best with all the plants growing to perfection.

It is a time for relaxation in the garden after attending to a variety of pleasant minor jobs - tidying the borders, dead heading the roses, watering and feeding the hanging baskets and other containers. It is so very important to pay attention to watering. Plants that are allowed to dry out can be seriously damaged for the remainder of the season and some may not recover. The cool of the evening is the best time to water your containers. The water will penetrate into the root area overnight with no loss due to evaporation. In very hot weather it may be necessary to water your plants twice daily. Keep to a regular feeding programme to sustain growth and flower production.

Don't forget the plants in the greenhouse which are at greater risk of drying out. It is best to get your plants out of the greenhouse and into a partly shaded area of the garden. You will find that your plants will grow much better in an open area where they are not scorched by the sun. It is particularly important to place your fuchsias and pelargoniums outdoors early in the summer for maximum growth.

A mulch around the base of trees and shrubs will conserve moisture and will greatly benefit the plants. Rapid growth will be sustained by providing inorganic fertilisers in granular form or as a liquid mix.

Planning Improvements

With more free time to relax in the garden it is worthwhile giving some serious thought to possible improvements to planting arrangements, general layout and to plants of particular merit which you may wish to add to your existing planting schemes. We should always aim to make the most of the space available.

It is worthwhile making a simple plan of the garden and the entire planting area. It may be found that some plants are in the wrong place and some may have out-grown their usefulness.

Get plants out of the greenhouse into a partly shaded area. Water plants in the cool of the evening.

Mixed Pansies - a massed planting can be quite impressive.

A colourful border featuring Pittisporum Irene Patterson, one of the finest for all year round colour.

23

Record on paper all the changes you would wish to make including new ideas for additional planting or the re-positioning of plants.

Make a point of visiting other gardens, garden centres, public parks and other plant display areas and note down those plants you would like to have in your own garden and their availability. Hold on to your notes and during summer and autumn give some thought to a simple plan of action to be taken during next winter and spring. Your plans need not be elaborate and do remember that any additional work can be carried out in easy stages.

The small to medium size garden can be transformed into a place of beauty with a little effort and at reasonable cost.

Weigela rubidor

Weigela rubidor - probably the most colourful of the Weigela family. Needs full sun.

Pinkie

A fragrant climbing rose and an excellent grower up to 3m. It can be trained as a shrub rose if pruned fairly hard late autumn·

Patios should be planted up with plenty of colourful flowers for maximum impact.

A partly open gate is an invitation to another part of Bob's garden. The ornamental gate in white can be a particularly attractive feature.

Some Pruning and Clearing

Late summer is here and for those of us who remain at home there is still lots of colour and beauty in the garden to enjoy.

This is a good time to do a little pruning. This light and simple task helps to keep shrubs compact. The removal of dead flowers will help to prevent energy sapping seed production. The available energy will go to improve next years flower display. Old branches that are exhausted and have served their purpose should be removed to allow more room for new vigorous shoots. Where pruning has been neglected for some years it is best to prune in stages over a few years i.e. a little pruning annually and cutting into live wood only. Hard pruning may be necessary if a shrub has become very overgrown and ungainly but should not be carried out as an annual routine. Remove spent flower heads from lilacs and rhododendrons. This will improve the appearance of the bushes and will encourage wood to ripen quite quickly thus improving next seasons display. Broom (cytisus), gorse (genista) and small shrubs like rock roses (cistus) should be pruned every year after flowering. Philadelphus, duetzias and weigelas should have their dead and very thin shoots and some of their flowering shoots - i.e. those which flowered this year - removed at ground level.

Mixed Floral arrangement

Spraying time

Roses should still be flowering well. Keep to a programme of spraying against blackspot and mildew. Regular foliar feeding with a liquid fertiliser is also recommended. On climbing and rambling roses tie in the new stems as they grow in length and train to the near horizontal position to produce flowering sub-laterals (side shoots). The old stems on the ramblers can be removed after they have finished flowering.

Dahlias will be at their best now. These glorious performers respond to granular or liquid feeding. Make sure that they do not run short of water. A good mulch of well rotted manure or compost will ensure a longer flowering period.

The flowering season for plants in hanging baskets and

Shrub rose Sally Holmes

This is a long flowering variety with mild fragrance.

other containers has still some weeks of colour left. Keep removing dead flowers and give the plants a liquid feed weekly. Your plants will also respond to foliar feeding. Fuchsias will be at peak performance now. Remove spent flowers as soon as they appear and keep on with regular high potash feeding. Spray against pests and keep the plants out of strong sun.

Lawn Care.

If the weather is very dry with high temperatures the mowing of the grass should be less frequent. When it is necessary to cut the grass in such conditions the cut should be raised. Keep the grass well watered and do this as darkness falls thus reducing loss by evaporation. There should be no further feeding with a high nitrogen fertiliser - mid-June is the latest.

Fuchsia Magellanica Aureus

Keep removing dead heads and treat plants to a liquid feed.

Pyracantha (Firethorn)

Climbing rose Ragtime -This recently introduced climber has a long flowering period. Flowers are a warm pink.

A section of Bob's garden in the late summer.

Winding down

The arrival of Autumn brings a complete change of colour to the garden. The crimson and gold foliage on the trees and the colourful display of berries set the scene for the decline in growth and the final stages in the flower border.

The annuals in the borders will be past their best in the next few weeks and when they are finally out of flower they should be removed to the compost heap. If the bedding plants in containers are still in flower they should be watered and fed to prolong their flowering period.

Grass sowing.

New grass should be sown by the end of the first week in September on soil that has been well prepared. Make sure that all weeds have been removed before sowing seed. This is also a good time to repair bare patches by raking the soil and scattering the seed. A light covering of the seed with fine peat will speed germination. Keep the newly sown areas moist until you see the new grass emerging through the soil and growing well.

The summer flowering heathers should be given a light clipping if they have finished flowering and at the same time add a top dressing of garden compost, fine bark chippings or the spent compost from your baskets or other containers.
Continue to feed fuchsias and remove dead flowers regularly before they set seed. Most fuchsias will now be at their peak flowering and will continue to flower until the end of autumn or early winter.

Bulbs for flowering early next year should be bought now if you wish to have the best selection.
Sweet pea seeds should be purchased now for sowing towards the end of October or early November. Seeds which are sown in pots and over-wintered in a cold frost free frame or greenhouse will produce well established plants for setting out in spring next year.
Sow the seeds 10 to 15 in a 15cm (6in) pot of potting compost and pinch out the tips when the plants are 15cm (6in) high.

September

Sweetpeas should be dead-headed promptly before they set seed.

Hertfordshire is a very fine, long flowering ground cover rose.

The bedding roses that have finished flowering can be cut back to prevent wind-rock. New beds should be prepared to receive the new roses which will be available end of November.

Roses planted into the ground in November will have made considerable growth before winter really sets in and they will have a head start over roses purchased and planted in spring next year.

Making a compost heap

This is a good time to make a compost heap. Very soon we will see the beginning of leaf fall from our deciduous trees and shrubs and we will also start on the removal of the summer bedding plants.

The perennials will be cut back in a month or two. All this valuable organic material, including grass clippings, kitchen waste (potato peelings, egg shells, tea bags etc.) can be used to make good compost. Organic material is anything that once lived, be it animal or vegetable. It is best to avoid any thick woody material as this can take a very long time to rot down.

Layers of lime or the specially formulated granular materials will speed up decomposition if they are applied to each 15cm (6in) layer of compost in the enclosure. It will take from 6 to 12 months to make a good quality compost.

Climbing roses or clematis, or both, will provide an impressive display of colour on an arch.

Escallonia Donard Seedling

This very fine evergreen bush makes an excellent hedge.

This peaceful Autumn setting is a reminder that the sap in the deciduous plants is slowing down and leaf fall will soon be under way. The end of another growing season is in sight and soon we will begin to plan for a new season of colour.

Adding Permanent Plants

The dying leaves of trees and shrubs in October gives a greater degree of colour intensity as they begin to fall to the ground and this is a clear sign that winter is not far away. It is a good time to give some thought to improvements in garden layout and to consider additional planting of colourful permanent plants.

The modern garden centres of today provide for sale an extensive range of trees and shrubs including evergreens with quite spectacular colourful foliage and suitable for large and small gardens.
These plants will give an excellent all year round display of golden, purple, copper or variegated foliage and many will surpass almost any floral display in the garden. The plants will already be growing in containers and can be planted out at any time of the year. They require very little attention and such plants are ideally suited for the retired person or those who are in business and have little spare time for gardening.
There is a great variety of colour variations throughout the four seasons. When considering the evergreens the heathers should not be overlooked. They are grown for their colourful display of foliage and flowers with the foliage giving a splendid display of colour all year.

There are two main groups - the Callunas and the Ericas. The Callunas flower mainly from mid-summer to late autumn. The largest group are the ericas and they have some species flowering in winter, spring and autumn. Some ericas are lime tolerant but it is best to grow all in humus rich acid soil which is free draining. An open sunny site suits them best. A well grown heather border can be quite a spectacle.

Careful planning is necessary when deciding what should be planted into the garden. Special consideration must be given to the ultimate size of the plant when it reaches maturity. It is best to list the plants you wish to have and to note their height and spread and other relevant details regarding position and soil type. As a general rule all lightly coloured and variegated foliage plants should be grown in an open position with good light.

Sorbus sargentii has wonderful autumn colour.

Crinodendron hookerianum

This evergreen plant produces red lantern-like flowers in early summer and into autumn. It requires a fertile to rich soil.

Winter protection of Fuchsias

To successfully over-winter your fuchsias (in pots or baskets) it is essential that they be kept in a frost free place and that they are not allowed to dry out completely.

The compost in the pot should be kept just slightly moist - not wet. Heat is not required for your mature plants i.e. those plants which are a year or more old.
The young plants which began life in the current year will need warmth and light to keep them ticking over until next spring - they will not have sufficient stamina to endure in a cold greenhouse.

The mature fuchsias can be over-wintered in a frost-free cold greenhouse, garden shed, garage, a cold room in the house, buried in peat in boxes (in their pots) or buried outside in trenches. Light is not required for your resting mature fuchsias.

Lawn Care

If moss has been a problem this year improve drainage by spiking. Scarify the lawn by raking with a grass rake to remove dead grass (thatch) and moss.

This is also an ideal time to apply an autumn lawn feed which will have essential nutritional elements to sustain and improve the grass for next year. The feed should be applied after the grass areas have been cleared of debris (leaves, fallen fruits, moss and thatch).

Robina Frisia Pseudoacacia

This beautiful deciduous small tree has very bright yellow foliage througout summer and to leaf-fall in late autumn.

Ilex Golden King (holly) - a fine evergreen shrub with red fruits later in the season.

Hebe Andersonii Variegatum

This is an excellent hebe with cream to light green foliage all year. It has a good display of pale pink flowers in summer. Place it in good light and in fertile soil.

Nature slowing down

The approach of the end of the autumn season brings shorter days and a drop in outside temperatures.

Most plants will be slowing down as the sap flow decreases and this is a sign that winter has arrived.

There are some jobs that should be started now. Sweep up leaves and place them on the compost heap. Clear footpaths and any other place where there are deposits of this valuable material. Mix the leaves with other organics such as grass clippings and household waste that does not contain fat, butter, cooking oil or any other greasy substance. The ground which is to be used for planting next year should be prepared now, if this task has not already been completed.

An ideal month to plant roses in their permanent position.

Start Planting

Trees and shrubs in liners or bare-rooted can be planted now if the weather is reasonable and frost is absent. This is also an ideal time to plant roses into their permanent positions.

All roses do really well when they are planted out before the end of November. The soil is still warm and this allows the plants to get off to a good start before winter takes hold.

Plants in the greenhouse may need a little heat now. Cold and damp conditions can cause fungae infections. Fuchsias and pelargoniums are vulnerable under such conditions. Ventilation is very important from now until spring. Keep air circulating and keep frost out of the greenhouse.

Philadelphus virginalis

Tulips should b planted out early this month so that they are well settled and into growth quickly to provide superb flowers next year.

Cut Back Chrysanths

The early flowering chrysanths will now have finished flowering and should be cut back to ground level. They can be left in the ground or potted up to over winter . This depends on the conditions in your garden and the hardiness of your plants. If in doubt they should be placed in the greenhouse.

Most of the herbaceous border will have dead or dying foliage. Cut back all the withered growth to ground level. This material can be stacked around the root area of your plants in the form of a mulch for root protection if you are in a frost area.

You may wish to place the material on the compost heap so that it is well rotted for use at planting out time next year.

Pieris forrestii (Forest flame)

This is one of the most popular evergreen plants. It is particularly colourful in spring and summer and it will give an excellent display of flowers when the plant matures. A good mulch of well rotted manure will pay dividends.

Cotoneaster

A reliable plant which will produce an abundance of fruits in autumn and winter.

Pittisporum Irene Patterson

This excellent evergreeen shrub gives a colourful display throughout the year.

Catalogue Time

This is the month for fireside gardening. In the next few weeks the seed catalogues will arrive and then the planning will begin with the help of the various gardening books.

Any garden notes that were made during last year should be reviewed and any desirable changes considered.

Seeds and young plants should be ordered as early as possible before stocks run short. There is a wide choice of seeds, plug plants and bulbs available and it is worthwhile trying some of the new introductions.

Propagation

There is still time to prepare the soil for planting in the New Year. New borders can be prepared now and old borders can be improved and made ready for new plants. Root cuttings from herbaceous perennials can be taken now to provide new plants for stocking the garden in the new year.

Suitable plants for easy propagation are Anthemis, papaver (poppy), verbascum, anchusa, phlox and gaillardia. Cut the large fleshy roots into 5cm (2in) pieces and pot them vertically into gritty compost. Make sure that they are positioned the right way up. The upper surface of the cutting should be just slightly above the compost in the pot. Lightly water the pots and place them in a cold frame or greenhouse.

Pipings can now be taken from perpetual flowering carnations. Remove 7.5cm (3in) long side shoots from the stems. Pull each shoot slightly upwards until it separates from the main stem and place it in gritty compost to half its length. Some warmth is necessary to ensure success - at least 10 degrees (50f.)

It is time to over-winter fuchsias and pelargoniums. The fuchsias will by now be past their best and ready for their winter rest. Cut your fuchsias back by about 1/3. Remove all flowers and foliage so that you are left with clean bare stems.

Cryptomeria Japonica Aureus (Japanese cedar).

A fast growing tree and evergreen - useful in the large garden. Golden foliage.

Remove all debris from the surface of the compost and leave the pot clean and tidy. Spray the stems and compost with an insecticide. Now place your resting fuchsias in a cool frost free place to over-winter. They must not be allowed to dry out - keep the compost just slightly moist. Check regularly to ensure that the compost has not dried out and that the plants have no pest problems. Light is not required when you are over-wintering mature fuchsias.

Pelargoniums require similar conditions to fuchsias during winter. Remove flowers and flower buds and cut away damaged stems and foliage. Keep the compost on the dry side and ensure that they are kept frost free.

Hedges and shrubs which have become bare at the base or too large for their allotted space can be pruned hard now. This entails cutting out one-third to one-half of the oldest shoots each winter for two or three years in succession.

Formal hedges that have grown too large or have been neglected can be rejuvenated by cutting back one face at a time. Allow the plants a year to recuperate between operations. Do not be tempted to prune too severely to ground level in one operation. The key to success is moderation i.e.- partial pruning over a number of years.

Thuga orientalis

An evergreen with bright foliage throughout the year.

A selection of evergreens suitable for the small garden.

Hebe Orphan Annie is well suited to container growing.

There is a great variety of hardy bulbs available and with a little planning we can have a glorious display of flowers in the garden for most of the year.

For each of the four seasons there are particular bulbs for providing seasonal colour. The greatest display of flowers from bulbs is in the spring. For the purpose of this article the term 'bulb' includes 'corms'.

The bulb has layers of fleshy material similar to an onion. It has storage organs at the base which is used for propagation. A corm is like a bulb but has solid flesh and a high content of starch.

Bulbs like a fertile growing medium which is rich in organic material. Where the soil is very heavy add a liberal supply of well rotted manure, sharp sand or grit and a good helping of bone meal. A few bulbs prefer planting in light shade but most do best in a warm, sunny position. They can be grown in the open ground or in containers. Good drainage is essential wherever they are grown.

The following varieties of flowering bulbs are recommended for their colourful range and for their hardiness:

Agapanthus (African Lily)

This plant has tall trumpet shaped blooms 7cm (2 1/2 in.) long from July to September and mostly blue. It is a superb plant for a sheltered sunny position. Cover the root area with a heavy mulch for winter protection.

Plants can be raised from seed in autumn or spring. Very slow to germinate seed. Best propagated from root division in spring.

Allium (The flowering onion)

Two types - dwarf alliums for the rockery and tall varieties for the back of the border. The variety A.giganteum is 1.2m (4ft) tall. This is a very good showy plant. Several varieties of bald-headed and tufted plants. Flowers from May to July. Requires full sun.

Can be grown from seed In autumn or from root division in spring or autumn.

The fine flowerheads of *Allium giganteum.*

Alstromeria (Peruvian Lily)

A superb plant which requires extra attention to get it to flower. Very good for the back of the border. Wide open flowers in attractive colours. Height 1m (3ft). A rich humus soil in full sun is necessary.

Propagate from fresh seed in autumn or divide root clump in spring.

Amaryllis (Belladona Lily)

The hardy amaryllis is very different from the large showy amaryllis which is grown indoors. Fragrant wide trumpet shaped flowers in pink blotched white are freely produced from September to early November. Height 60cm (2ft). Well drained soil is essential.

Increase by division in spring or late summer.

Belladonna Lily

Anemone

There is a very large family of anemone and there is an enormous range of colours and heights. It is a plant worth growing if continuity of flowering is required. There are singles, semi-doubles and doubles and they vary in size from 15cm (6in) to 1.2m (4ft) high. Flowering period is from February to September according to variety.
They prefer a sunny or a semi-shaded aspect.

Arum (Cuckoo Pint)

The arum is a particularly useful plant and it is at home in the border, the rockery and in a woodland setting. The flowers can be a spadix (i.e. a fleshy spike in which small flowers are embedded) or a spathe (i.e. a brack surrounding an infloresence). This is a very eye-catching plant in colours of red and yellow. Humus rich soil in sun or light shade suits them best. Height 22cm (9in) to 45cm(18in). Flowering period June and July.

Offset tubers can be removed in autumn and potted up. Whole clumps can also be divided in autumn.

Anemone

Begonia

There is an extremely wide range of begonias - fibrous rooted and tuberous varieties. They are succulent (fleshy) and they have a long flowering period. The range of colours is vast and they can be single or semi double. They are not hardy and are mentioned here because they are such an accommodating plant for garden cultivation through summer and into autumn. Begonias can be planted into the open ground when all danger of frost has passed. Lift tubers before winter frosts and store in a frost free place to over winter.

Tubers can be divided with an 'eye' on each section and planted up in autumn or spring. For early results it is best to buy whole tubers.

Begonia nonstop variety

Camassia (Quamash)

This is a most attractive plant for a woodland or grassland situation. Tall floral spikes up to 1 m (3ft 3in) high appear late May and into July - varieties with white and blue flowers. Likes sun and semi-shade.

They are very slow from seed and erratic. It is best to lift, divide and plant out root divisions in autumn.

Canna (Canna Lily)

This is a must for those who have a well sheltered garden in full sun. The plant dislikes cold winds and severe frost. Cannas are a most attractive plant with brightly coloured blooms and colourful foliage. Red or orange flowers splashed yellow and purple foliage. The leaves are paddle shaped and 30cm (1ft) long. A humus rich soil in full sun is essential. Cut rhizomes into sections in spring and plant out.

Seed can be sown in autumn at 20 degrees (68f.) for spring planting.

Camassia - a colourful herbaceous perennial.

Colchicum (Autumn chorus)

This plant is not related to the true crocus. The upright tubular flowers appear from September to November. Several varieties 15cm (6in) high in pink, violet and white. It can be depended upon to provide a beautiful carpet of flowers in autumn. A humus rich soil in light shade suits them best.
Propagate by seed or division in autumn.

Colchicum

Crocosmia (montbretia)

An important garden plant for the mixed herbaceous border. Superb sword-like leaves and an extensive flower spike with small tubular blooms. Flowers are red, orange and yellow. The variety c. lucifer has very bright red flowers and is particularly attractive. Height up to 90cm (3ft). The flowering period is from July to September. A humus rich soil and bone meal will give excellent results.

Crocus

This plant has a range of flower shapes with some varieties flowering at different times of the year. There are three principal groups 7-12cm (3-4in) high. The very early crocus flower from February to March - 7cm (3in) high and are mostly yellow. The spring varieties flower February to April. The autumn flowering types flowers from September to December. The colours are yellow, blue, gold and violet. The planting area must be well drained. They will do well in sun or light shade.
Propagate in early autumn by seed or divide clumps after flowering.

Crocus

Cyclamen

A most rewarding plant for the shaded part of the garden. The flowering periods are January to March, July to September and September to November. The earliest variety to grow is c. hederifolium - the ivy leafed variety which is pink and white and flowers from September to November. Cyclamen require a soil which is rich in organic matter and a situation which is in shade.
Propagate by sowing seeds in spring and plant out in autumn.

Cyclamen

Fritillaria

The garden fritillaria has tall stems with bell-shaped flowers in yellow, red and orange. The variety acmopetala is particularly good for the mixed border. It is 45cm (1 1/2 ft) high and has purple flowers with yellow stripes. The flowering period is from April to June. A well drained soil in partial shade suits them well.

Propagate by offsets in summer or by seed in autumn.

Galanthus (Snowdrops)

These small white flowered plants make a wonderful carpet of colour in January and they flower right through to late March. Height is only 15cm (6in). The variety G.S. Arnott is large flowered and fragrant and is probably the best hybrid. Moist humus rich soil and a shaded aspect suits them best.

For best results propagate by division in spring after flowering (plants in green leaf). Can also be divided in late summer or autumn when bulbs are dormant.

Galanthus (snowdrops)

Gladiolus (Sword Lily)

There is a very wide choice of gladiola varieties and there are several groups to choose from. They come in a great variety of heights from 45cm (1 1/2 ft) to 1.2cm (4ft). The taller varieties need to be staked. The flowers on the stalk vary in size from 10 - 17cm (4 -7in) and are classified giant, large, medium, small and miniature. The colour range is vast. A fertile soil with some garden compost and a sunny position will give excellent results.

Propagate by seed or by removal of young cormlets from parent plants after lifting . Place cormlets in a frost free place and plant out in spring 5cm (2in) deep. Flowers from cormlets will take 3 years. Seed sown in early spring will also take approx three years to flower.

Hyacinthus

The hyacinth is one of the most delightful plants in the garden in late spring. The flower heads are packed close with masses of small flowers and all have a very strong fragrance. The most popular are the Dutch varieties. The colour range is vast. Hyacinths require a moist humus rich soil in sun or light shade.

Remove offsets at lifting time and pot up to grow on. Plant out in autumn.

Hyacinth

Iris

There are two groups - the rhizome group and the bulb group. The bearded irises are very popular and they belong to the rhizome group. There is a very extensive range of irises in both groups and it is really a matter of personal taste. The bulb group are smaller and they are suited to the rockery.

There are wide variations in the flowering period..Some of the rhizome group flower March to May. The winter varieties flower between November and March. Many in the bulb group also flower in winter. A well drained sandy soil and full sun is necessary for all irises. Heights vary between 30cm -60cm (1ft -2ft).

Propagate species by division of rhizomes or offsets in late summer or by seed in autumn. Named cultivars will not come true from seed.

Lilium (Lily)

The lily is quite an exotic plant with a tremendous range of colours and with heights ranging from dwarfs at 30cm (1ft) to giants at 2.5m (8ft). The flowers are large and have three principal shapes - Turk's cap. The petals are reflected. The trumpet shaped lilies and the bowl shaped varieties are the most common. Lilies require a well drained site with lots of well rotted manure and bone meal. Full sun is essential. The plants also do very well in large containers with free drainage.

Propagate by seed in autumn or spring, by bulb scales in summer or by stem bulbils in autumn.

Lilium

Narcissus (Daffodil)

There is an almost endless list of varieties of Narcissi with colourful trumpet shaped flowers at various heights. The colour range is extensive.
They are ideal for naturalising (i.e. planting them in woodland or grassland and allowing them to grow and increase naturally without disturbance). Yellow predominates.
The narcissus family do very well in containers, rockeries and the edges of beds - the dwarf varieties are particularly suitable for this purpose. A well drained soil with organic material in sun or partial shade suits them best.

These plants will increase naturally by offsets they produce. Clumps can be divided eight weeks after flowering. Species can be grown from fresh seed in late summer or autumn.

Nerine

Nerine bowdenii

The hardy variety is N.bowdenii and it is an excellent late autumn flowering plant massed with wide funnel shaped flowers from September to October. They require a humus rich soil in a sheltered part of the garden and a position in full sun. Height is 60cm (2ft). Nerines resent root disturbance.

Propagate from fresh seed sown in November. Offsets can be removed in late autumn when plants have died back. Pot up and plant out in Spring.

Bob's Gardening Clinic

O ver the years in addressing groups across the province, and with the many visitors to his own showpiece garden, Bob Brooks has been asked numerous questions on general cultivation and the care of garden plants. *Here he lists some of the most common problems and his answers to the questions posed:-*

Q. - My climbing rose 'Compassion' produces only a few flowers at the top of the plant. How can I get the plant to be more floriferous?

A. - It is best to train the lateral stems of climbing roses to the horizontal position. Fan shaped growth is ideal. Sap from the roots must go up and it will rush to the top area of the plant to produce flowers. By training the stems near to the horizontal and fan shaped the sap will still force its way upwards and will do so by producing flowering side shoots (sub-laterals) all the way along the lateral stems. These new flowering side shoots will appear every 10cms (4ins) along the stems and there will be lots of them and all eager to flower. The climbing rose that has been trained as outlined above will produce a massive display of flowers throughout summer providing the plant has been well fed to sustain growth.

Climbing roses are best pruned after they have finished flowering - ie, usually November or early December. Exhausted stems should be removed and the flowering sub-laterals, which will be longer by now, should be reduced to 15cm (6ins). Tie the stems to the trellis or other support.

Provide a good 15cm (6in) thick mulch at the root area and feed with a liquid or granular fertiliser in mid-February. Foliar feeding twice weekly from February to September works wonders. A further granular feed in mid-June will sustain growth and flowers through summer and autumn.

Graham Thomas

Ritter Von Barmstedt - An attractive horizontal trained climbing rose.

Q. - Is there anything to be gained by using cloches?

A. - If you have enough cloches you can have an early supply of lettuce, spring onions, carrots, raddish etc.

Place the cloches over the prepared soil in the plot at least a week before sowing the seed. This will raise the temperature of the soil quite quickly and allow seeds to be sown early. The seeds will germinate within a few weeks, depending on outside temperature.

Q. - When is the best time to apply chemical (granular) fertilisers to my roses, clematis, trees and shrubs?

A - Granular fertilisers depend on the rain breaking the material down and leaching the nutrients to the roots of plants. With average rainfall this takes approx. six weeks.

If the granules are applied to the root area surface in mid-February the nutrients will be down at the roots by early April and ready to be carried up through the plants vascular system to the foliage. Each leaf is a miniature factory and it is the leaves which convert the sap and its nutrients into complex foods through the process of photosynthesis (i.e. - conversion of raw nutrients to plant food by light).

The foods produced by the foliage are passed through the stems to various parts of the plant to produce flowers, foliage and fruit - this process consumes approx. 50% of the manufactured food. The remaining 50% goes towards extending the root system.
It is obviously important to keep the foliage healthy and the roots fed.

Mixed rose bush

Generous feeding is important.

Q. - What is meant by softwood and hardwood cuttings?

A. - A softwood cutting is taken from new growth early on in the growing season when the cutting is young, succulent, vibrant and full of sap. Such cuttings are full of energy and they root quite quickly. This is an easy cutting to root and the young plant has all spring, summer and all autumn to develop its roots, to mature and become established before the onslaught of winter. A softwood or semi-ripe cutting taken later on in the season will still be immature by winter and will require nursing with bottom heat to get it through the winter months.

A hardwood cutting is taken from a mature plant in late summer or autumn. In most cases hardwood cuttings are quite hardy and many will survive outdoors in winter. Growth is quite slow.
Softwood cuttings are more reliable and are usually the best choice.
It should be noted that hardwood cuttings should be taken only when the sap is up (i.e. in flow). There is no point in taking a cutting when the sap is down as there is little energy in the stem and therefore the plant has no desire to produce a root - the plant is at rest.

A typical herbaceous border.

Q. - When is the best time to divide herbaceous perennials?

A. - Hardy perennials such as geraniums (cranesbill), anthemis, shasta daisies, gaillardia, helianthemum etc. can be removed from the ground in mild weather, i.e. in autumn or spring, and divided.   Take sections of the root clump from the outer edges of the plant and discard the centre portion. Break off a piece of the plant preferably with a stem which has a piece of root attached to it. This new portion can be planted right away into fresh soil in the border or potted up and placed in the greenhouse to grow on for planting out next year.
 An early autumn planting into fertile fresh soil followed by a reasonably mild winter will ensure a well grown plant by the following spring.

Q. - What are the ideal conditions for seed sowing in the open ground in spring?

A. - A well prepared soil which has been cleared of perennial and annual weeds and a soil that is fertile and in good heart will give the best results. Mild weather and frost free conditions are also important.
Do not sow out seeds too early. Follow the chickweed sign.
Chickweed is a fussy plant and it will only grow on soil that is fertile and in good heart. It appears above ground only when the temperature is right. When you see the chickweed appearing it is time to sow your seeds.
Remove the chickweed and sow you seeds for successful germination.

— · — · — · — · — · —

Q. - I find it difficult knowing when to prune my flowering shrubs.

A. - The general rule is that shrubs which flower in summer or autumn on the current season's newly produced wood, i.e. flowers produced on the tips of shoots (or stems produced earlier in the same year) are pruned hard in early spring.
These will include buddleias, large flowered (H.T.) and cluster flowered (FLOR) roses, caryopteris, hardy fuchsias and some clematis.

Shrubs which flower in summer on the previous year's growth should be pruned after they have finished flowering. This group includes flowering currents, forsythias, philadelphus,kolkwitzias and weigelas.
Remove the stems that have flowered and leave the fresh new stems for flowering next year.

— · — · — · — · — · —

Follow the chickweed sign for sowing.

A simple patio arrangement.

Q. - Rabbits keep eating my herbaceous perennials.
I would like to grow a few plants that they will not eat.

A. - There is a rather limited variety of plants that rabbits
will not eat. The following list of plants are known to be
off their menu.

Acanthus Mollis (Dutchman's breeches) - This is a tall
showy plant up to 1.5m (5ft.) high. Well furnished with
spikes of pink and white flowers all summer.
Aconitum (Monkshood) This is also an attractive tall
growing plant up to 1m. (3ft.) high. There are several varieties all in shades of blue. The flowers resemble monks
with their hoods on and the hoods are removable.
Alchemilla Mollis (Lady's Mantle) Very pale green to
yellow foliage and yellow flowers in summer.
Aquilegia (Columbine) This is a good cottage plant.
Various cultivars; open throated, bi-coloured flowers in
summer 35cm (14ins.) high.
Digitalis (Foxglove) There is a very large group of fox-
gloves. Pendulous, tubular flowers in summer. Height
1.2m (4ft.).
Euphorbia (Spurge) Several varieties in colour over a
long period in summer. The bracts can be red, golden
yellow, light green or a mix of these colours.. Height
50cm (20in.).
Heleborous. There are several superb cultivars and they
flower at different times of the year. H. niger (The
Christmas Rose) is very popular. Height 35cm (14 in.).
Iris. The stems and the spikey leaves are as tough as
old boots and difficult for a rabbit to get its teeth into.
Best planted in groups of 3,5,7 etc for a colourful display.
Lupins Tall spikes of very colourful flowers in summer.
They take up a lot of space. Height up to 1.2m (4ft.).

If you plant out the above named perennials your rabbit
intruders will get the 'cold shoulder' and move on.

Plants that give rabbits
'the cold shoulder'.

Digitalis (Foxglove)

Garden Centres and Nurseries
supporting this publication as part sponsors

BALLYLESSON GARDEN CENTRE
148 Ballylesson Road, Belfast, BT8 8JU
Tel (028) 9082 6467 Fax (028) 9082 6231
Visit our website:
www.cameronlandscapes.com

BRAESIDE NURSERY
25 School Road, Crossnacreevy,
Castlereagh, Belfast, BT5 7UA
Tel (028) 9044 8426
www.braesidenursery.co.uk

COLEMANS GARDEN CENTRE
6 Old Ballyclare Road, Templepatrick
BT39 0BJ,
Tel. (028) 9443 2513 Fax (028) 9443 2151
info@colemansgardencentre.co.uk

COLERAINE GARDEN CENTRE,
255 Dunhill Rd, Coleraine, BT51 3QJ,
Tel: (028) 7035 7972

HAMILTONS AT DICKSON GARDEN CENTRE
79 Cootehall Road, Bangor,
BT19 1UP Tel (028) 9185 3397
            Fax (028) 9185 2779
www.dicksonsgardencentre.co.uk

HILLSIDE NURSERY CENTRE
328 Doagh Road, Newtownabbey, Co. Antrim,
BT36 6XL Tel: (028) 9086 3161
            Fax: (028) 9086 5666
www.hillsidenurserycentre.co.uk

KYLESTONE NURSERIES,
5 Lower Balloo Rd., Groomsport,
Bangor,
Tel/Fax: 9188 3989,
Mob: 07796 614914

THE LANDSCAPE CENTRE,
24 Donegore Hill, Dunadry , Antrim BT41 2QU
Tel: (028) 9443 2175 Fax (028) 9443 2051
www.landscape-centre.com

LOGWOOD MILL GARDEN CENTRE
8 Logwood Road, Ballyclare BT39 9LR
Tel. (028) 9332 2242 Fax (028) 9334 9020
www logwoodmillgc.co.uk

NESS GARDEN CENTRE
234 Glenshane Road, Londonderry,
BT47 3SN Tel (028) 7130 1285
Visit:www.nessnurseries.co.uk
Gift tokens, Coffee shop, Florist shop, Gift shop.

POTS OF PLEASURE
13 The Square, Ballyclare BT39 9BB
Tel/Fax (028) 9334 0903
Container gardening and giftware specialists.

SAINTFIELD NURSERIES
88 Belfast Road BT24 7HE,
Tel (028) 9081 4331
Fax (028) 9081 5084
www.saintfieldnurseries.co.uk

SAMORE PLANT CENTRE
135 Glenravel Road,Martinstown ,
Ballymena BT43 6QW
Tel (028) 2175 8627 Fax (028) 2175 9998

SUNNYBANK GARDEN CENTRE
48 Beltoy Road, Carrickfergus
BT38 9BH   Tel (028) 9335 1558
            Fax (028) 9336 828

Roses are the most popular choice when gardeners are planning the creation of a fragrant flower border. It is important to remember that they thrive in a sunny aspect. They will tolerate a position in light shade for part of the day but in order to grow them really well they need several hours of full sun.

A south facing position and shelter from cold winds is ideal and this will greatly enhance the potential fragrance. In walled gardens and where rosebeds are surrounded by hedges their fragrance is held captive and on a warm calm evening the fragrance can be quite pronounced.

There is an almost endless list of fragrant roses and the most fragrant are the hybrid teas (large flowered) and the gallicas, the alba roses, the damask group, moss and the hybrid musks. In garden centres at this time of the year there is usually a good variety of quality roses in liners and they can be planted at any time of the year but preferably between November and March.

The following short list of popular hybrid tea roses have superb fragrance and they can be relied upon to grow well and to flower in their season.
Eden Rose is a recent introduction. It is a robust plant with large deep pink fragrant flowers. Height 1m(3ft.)
Champion has very large cream/golden yellow flowers flushed pink and a strong sweet fragrance. Height 1m. (3ft.)
Alec's Red - this is an old McGredy rose with a good reputation for free flowering and good disease resistance. The fragrance is very pleasant and quite pronounced. Height 1m (3ft.).
Josephine Bruce is an old well cultivated favourite with very dark red velvet flowers and a wonderful fragrance. Height 60cm (2ft.).
Mr Lincoln - this very popular rose has dark red flowers and a very sweet fragrance. Height 1m. (3ft.).
Mojave - this is a new rose with flowers in warm orange against glossy dark green foliage. It is a vigorous and reliable rose with a strong fragrance. Height 1m. (3ft.)
Mullard Jubilee has great vigour and it is a reliable old favourite. The flowers are red and very large with a strong fragrance Height 60cm (2ft.).

Roses
The fragrant choice

Paul Shirville - large flowered HT.

Scepter'd Isle

Paul Shirville is very vigorous with salmon pink flowers which are very fragrant. It is a very popular rose . Height 1m.

The floribunda roses (cluster flowered) have flowers not quite as large or as shapely as the hybrid teas but they are generally more floriferous and they tend to flower continuously rather than the distinct short flushes of the hybrid tea roses. Only a few have the strong fragrance of the tea roses.

The following floribundas are recommended for their fragrance and flower quality.:

Remember Me (hybrid tea)

Apricot Nectar has apricot/yellow flowers which are very fragrant. Height 1m.

Escapade - this very attractive rose has single flowers in cerise violet. A very good grower. Height 1.2m (4ft.)

Margaret Merril - a great favourite with rosarians. Small white flowers all summer long and with very strong fragrance. It is never out of flower in its season. Height 60cm (2ft.).

Rose of Tralee - this old McGredy variety has fully double pink suffused white flowers and a superb fragrance. It flowers all summer if well fed. Height 75cm (21/2ft.).

Samaritan - named for the Samaritan Society. This is a new rose with large apricot flowers and a delightful fragrance. Lots of flowers all summer. Height 75cm (21/2 ft.)

The Polyantha - pompon roses are bushy, compact plants with summer long flowering up to 1m (3ft.) high. Most have a very sweet fragrance. This large group is worth considering where space is limited.

Climbing roses are essential in any rose garden planting scheme. They have various scents with many quite outstanding and they are particularly suitable for the back of the rose border.

Ritter Von Barmstedt

Fascinating Fuchsias

Fuchsias are gaining in popularity at an alarming rate and this is understandable when you consider how easy they are to grow and the wide choice of cultivars (cultivated varieties) available today.

At present there are over 4,000 different varieties of fuchsias and about 250 hardy types. You can have a stunning and long flowering display of colourful fuchsias in hanging baskets, window boxes, pots and other containers and you can also create borders by using hardy bedding cultivars. The bush fuchsias have upright growth and the basket types are pendulous or trailing. There are double flowering, semi-double and single flowering fuchsias. It is really a matter of personal choice when it comes to deciding which to grow. A visit to fuchsia shows and other fuchsia display areas will help you to decide. Take a pencil and notebook with you and do not be afraid to ask questions.

The cultivation of fuchsia is quite easy and I think that it is best to grow just as many as you can manage without too much difficulty. There is no point in having a vast amount of fuchsias with most of them neglected and in poor condition. It is best to have a smaller number well cared for, in good health, producing lots of flowers and easily managed.

From mid-spring your fuchsias will grow quite vigorously. If the tips are stopped (pinchcd out) you should have a glorious display of flowers. It is essential to keep the plants reasonably cool and it is best to place them outdoors from mid June when all danger of frost has passed.

They must never be allowed to dry out and they should have regular liquid feeding with a high potash fertiliser. A tomato fertiliser will give excellent results. Weekly feeding is recommended and in accordance with the manufacturers directions. Many fuchsia growers prefer quarter strength at every watering rather than a full strength application weekly. I find that the quarter strength at every watering gives me excellent results.

Continue to remove spent flowers before they set seed and this will conserve the plants energy and will help to produce more flowers.

Mission bells - a delightful bush variety.

Pests

Keep a look out for pests on your fuchsias and spray regularly with a good insecticide. Greenfly and whitefly can be a problem in summer and it is very important that they be kept under control.

Bedding Fuchsias

If you have a surplus of fuchsias in pots you may wish to plant them into your border for summer display only. A position out of full sun suits them best. Make a planting hole the size of the pot and place the pot and the fuchsia into the hole and leave it there to flower. Continue with watering and feeding.

Your plant can be safely left in this position until the end of September when it should be removed to a frost-free place for overwintering.

Hardy Fuchsias

There are 250 varieties of hardy fuchsias and many of them are quite exceptional and worthy of a permanent place in the garden where they will flower all summer long until the frost cuts them down. The hardies are very much under-rated and should be more widely grown.

They are not fussy about position and will do very well facing north, west or east. They prefer a fertile soil and it is therefore best to add plenty of well rotted manure or compost at the root area and some bone meal. Ensure that your plant is mature i.e. it should be in a 150 mm pot and the pot full of roots.

There is no point in planting a hardy which is little more than a seedling - it would not survive its first winter. It is best to plant your hardy in the spring thus ensuring its establishment and a reasonably good root system before winter.

Devonshire Dumpling
This is a fine basket type fuchsia.

Lena Dalton

When you have prepared the planting hole remove the plant from its pot and place it in the planting hole 10 cm (4ins) below ground level. This deeper planting will give your fuchsia considerable protection against frost in its first and future years.

Place a heavy mulch of well rotted manure or compost around the surface of the root area before winter. This insulator can be removed in spring to reveal the new basal growth. Last years old flowering stems should be cut back to ground level at this time. Regular liquid feeding will ensure a long flowering display.

The following hardy fuchsias are highly recommended for their superb performance throughout summer. There are lots more to choose from and these can be seen in your garden centre and at fuchsia shows:

Alice Hoffman

Alice Hoffman - semi-double rose/white flowers from late June.good growth. Height 60 cm x 40 cm spread. Long flowering.

Genii - small single flowers are cerise/purple. Superb golden yellow foliage; needs full sun. Very long flowering period. Height 60cm x 30cm spread. Probably the most popular of the hardies. Will do well in a container. A good choice.

Madam Cornellison - this one is a very strong plant with rich scarlet/white flowers all summer and into autumn. Height 76cm x 45cm spread.

Megellanica Aureus - this is a very strong growing plant up to 2 m height x 1.5 m spread. Best at the back of the border and in full sun. Bright yellow foliage and scarlet/purple flowers all summer and well into autumn.

Mrs Popple - a strong growing plant up to 75 cm high x 40 cm spread. Dark green foliage; small red/purple flowers. A very popular variety.

.

Paula Jane

The Clematis family is a large one and there is quite an impressive range of species and hybrids, evergreen and deciduous, widely available. The clematis is not a demanding plant. They are easy to grow and most are hardy. Feed them well and give them plenty of water and you will be rewarded with a wonderful display of colourful flowers in their season. Large and small flowered varieties are available and the colour range is vast.

Clematis are not only valuable climbing plants, they can also be used for ground cover in prostrate form and are particularly attractive when seen cascading down slopes and banks. Choose the mid and late summer flowering varieties for such schemes. These varieties can also be used to scramble over balconies and will cascade downwards with a stunning display of colour to about 3 metres (l0ft). The small flowered vitacellas are particularly suitable if you wish to have a more extensive drop.

Take care to ensure that the flower colour will contrast with the balcony backdrop, e.g. - a red or blue flowered clematis seen against a white or other light coloured background is very attractive. Use a large container for your clematis, at least 40cms wide by 40cms deep (16in. x 16in.), and ensure that there are sufficient drainage holes - use crocks to aid drainage. They do best in John Innes soil based compost No 3. Place the container behind the balcony wall or railings out of sight and train the stems over and down to cascade.

Clematis of your choice can be planted into the garden and into containers as soon as the weather is reasonably settled - plant out by the Spring. It is quite a simple task to plan and to plant varieties of clematis which will flower in succession for about 10 months of the year.

Choose those varieties which will come into flower when another has finished. Plants for sale have labels attached with printed instructions regarding site position, height, flowering time, colour and pruning advice

Barbara Dibley

This is a Group 2 large flowered hybrid and flowers May and June and again in September. It requires only light pruning after it finishes flowering.

There are three principal groups of clematis and within each of these groups there are several minor groups of named varieties. The principal groups are numbered 1,2, and 3 and this indicates the sequence of their flowering period. By selecting clematis from each of these groups you can be sure of a continuous display of colour throughout most of the year.

Group 1 Clematis are the early flowering varieties and they flower between January and May. This is quite a large group and includes seven minor groups - the evergreen Chrysocomas, Cirrhosas, Armandii varieties and the single "Cartmanii Joe" plus the deciduous Alpinas, Macropetalas and the Montanas.

The evergreen clematis flower between January and April. They are quite vigorous with the exception of Cartmanii Joe which grows to only 1.5 metres high. This is a superb rockery clematis flowering in April. It is quite floriferous and is sweetly scented.

The Alpinas have bell shaped flowers mostly in blue. The variety 'Francis Rivis' has mid-blue flowers and is very popular. The variety 'Alpinus Ruby' has rich red flowers with white stamens and is also very popular. The Alpinas flower in April.

The Macropetalas flower late April/early May and they have nodding bell-shaped flowers in blue, red and pink. The varieties 'Maidwell Hall' - deep blue flowers and 'Markhamii' (Markhams pink) are firm favourites in this minor group.

The last of the early flowering clematis to flower are the Montanas (Flower of the Mountain) and they put on their glorious display in May and into June. This is the largest group within Group 1 and some are very vigorous and will grow to 10 metres. The Group 1 early flowering clematis do not require regular pruning and can be left to flower year after year. Pruning will be necessary only if the plant has outgrown its allotted space or if, after a number of years, it has accumulated an excessive amount of dead wood. If pruning becomes necessary, it should be carried out immediately the plant finishes flowering and before it has started to produce new wood for flowering the following year.

Elsa Spath - Group 2, flowering period June to September. Lightly prune after flowering.

Louise Rowe: Group 2 - flowers June, July and September. Pruning is optional.

The Group 2 clematis are the next to flower. These are large flowered hybrids and they come into flower late May/early June. This is also a very extensive Group with a very wide choice of wonderful colours including bi-coloured, multi coloured and double varieties, Among the most popular in this group we have:

Barbara Dibley - Flowers are violet with deep carmine bars. Dark stamens. Vibrant.

Beauty of Worcester - Double blue variety - white centre.

Dr Rupple - Rosemadder with deep carmine bar. Golden stamens.

Elsa Spath (A.K.A XERXES) - Deep violet blue with purple shadings. Very large flowers.

H.F Young - Wedgwood blue with cream stamens. Said to be the best blue.

Louise Rowe - Wedgwood Blue with cream stamens. Double flowered. Superb variety.

Mrs M Thompson - Deep violet with vivid scarlet bar. Striking colour.

Nellie Moser - Mauve pink with deep carmine bar. Very popular.
Most of the clematis in this Group will flower for about 8 weeks and most will produce a second flush in Autumn. They produce their flowers on the old and the new wood and require only light pruning in February when dead wood should be removed. At the same time prune each live stem down by about 30cms (12 ins.) to two fat buds at a node. This treatment will ensure lots of new growth and flowers.

Group 3 Clematis are the last to flower and they commence in early July. Some will continue into October/November if the weather is reasonably mild. In this group we have the minor groups of Jackmanii, the Vitacellas, the Texensis, the Orientalis and the herbaceous clematis.

Kathleen Dunfold / William Kennett Group 2 varieties and in flower May, June and September.

Rhederiana a yellow vigorous and fragrant variety. Height up to 6m (18ft) and in flower from August to October.

The Vitacellas and the Orientalis varieties deserve a special comment. Both are extremely free flowering, very reliable and trouble free. The Vitacellas are particularly floriferous with flowers 5cm wide and star shaped. Various colours are available - deep purple, majenta, and reds predominate.

The most popular Vitacellas are
Abundance - Flowers are 5cm wide. Bright red. Very free flowering.
Alba Luxurins - Pure white variety with yellow stamens. Vigorous.
Etoile Violette - Bell shaped flowers. Strong violet colour. Vigorous.
Madam Julia Correvon - Red flowers 5cms wide and star shaped. Very long flowering period.
Margot Koster - Small red flowers 5cm wide. Very free flowering.
Purpurea Plena Elegans - Rosette shaped, violet purple double flowers. Very free flowering. Very vivid against a light background.
Royal Velors - Royal purple. The deepest purple of this group.
The flowers of the Orientalis varieties are bell shaped, yellow and pendulous. They produce very attractive silver seed heads when they finish flowering.

The most popular Orientalis Clematis are:
Bill MacKenzie - Large yellow bell shaped flowers. Very vigorous and long flowering. Starts to flower mid August.
Orientalis - Medium yellow bell shaped flowers. Long flowering.
Rhederiana - Primrose yellow with purple stamens.
Fragrant Serratifolia - Pale yellow nodding flowers with purple stamens (AKA Koreana).
Tangutica Gravetye - Yellow flowers, lantern shaped. Very vigorous.
Pruning of the Vitacellas and the Orientalis varieties is not necessary. If these varieties are used to cover sheds, fences or for climbing trees, they can be left to climb naturally. If space is limited they can be pruned hard in February.   All the other Group 3 clematis must be pruned hard to 30 cms (12 ins) February.

Montana tetrarose - Group 1 early flowering.

Macropetela markhamii (Markham's pink) - Group 1, early flowering.

Cornus
Contraversa
Aureus

Trees and Shrubs

Trees and shrubs add life to a garden. They are a focal point and bring colourful foliage changes as one season follows another. When planning a planting scheme for the small garden it is essential to include a few small trees and shrubs.

A garden, however small, is incomplete without a tree. A tree grown as a specimen plant at the far end of the garden will draw the eye of the visitor. The beauty of the tree in form, foliage and in flower will be particularly attractive.

Consider framing a striking distant view with trees and shrubs.   Use them to screen obtrusive buildings. Walk around the garden and look at all viewing aspects including views when approaching the house. A mental picture of the tree or shrub of your choice in situ will help you to make the right decision.

The principal considerations when choosing trees are size and growth rate, habit and foliage and possible encroachment onto your neighbours property. Keep your tree well clear of your neighbours boundary wall or fence and take care to avoid drains, water mains and underground cables.

It is also important to keep trees clear of windows and external doors so that there is no restrictive view of the garden from inside the house.

Syringa

Acer palmatum
atropurpureum

Sites for new trees should be prepared in the autumn or winter for planting in the spring. Dig a hole at least 40cm deep and 40cm wide (16ins x 16ins) then fork over the bottom of the hole to ensure efficient drainage. Work in plenty of well rotted manure, garden compost or peat and add a good handful of bonemeal to the mix. Leave to settle before planting.

If the tree to be planted is bare rooted make sure that the hole is wide enough take the fully spread out roots. Container trees can be planted at any time of the year but are best planted November to March.

The following list of trees briefly describe those which are suitable for the small gardens. Acers are very attractive when in leaf. They require acid soil and an area sheltered from cold winds. They are all deciduous.

Acer Japonicum Aureum

This Japanese maple is very attractive with its magnificent golden yellow foliage in spring and summer. When mature it produces masses of small red flowers which contrast significantly with the foliage. It is very slow growing but will eventually reach 3m with a spread of 3m (l0ft. x 10ft).

Chamecyparis lawsoniana columnaris

This fastigiate Lawsons Cypress requires very little space. The foliage is blueish on undersides and tips. Height 4.5m (15ft) spread is only 60cm (2ft).

Cornus mas

The cornelian cherry has tiny yellow flowers in great profusion and carried on the leafless stems in winter. The flowers are followed by red fruits. In the autumn the foliage is rich red. This is a very graceful tree. Height 4..5m spread 4.5m (15ft x 15ft).

Crataegus lavallei

Also known as C. carrierei. This small tree produces white flowers in late spring and into early summer. It is deciduous but the foliage remains on the tree until late winter. The autumn foliage is red with red haws which remain well into winter. Height 4.5 spread 3m (15ft x 10ft).

Cydonia oblonga

This is an old fashioned tree for the typical cottage garden. White flowers in spring are followed by pear-shaped fruits which are strongly scented. Foliage turns yellow in autumn. Soil must be fertile to rich. Needs full sun and shelter. Height 4.5m. Spread 3.5m (15ft x 12ft).

Ficus Carica -

Acer Japonicum Aurem

Ozothamnus, rosmarinifolius

This splendid summer flowering evegreen shrub requires full sun and well drained soil.

The edible fig is a superb spreading tree. No flowers but large lobed leaves which are very attractive. Needs to have its roots restricted to encourage fruiting. Best planted in a container above or below soil level. Not suitable for exposed gardens. Height 3m., spread 3m. (l0ft x 10ft).

Ilexaquifolium argenteomarginata pendula -
With a name like this it would need to be a good one. Perry's silver weeping holly is a superb elegant small tree. Green leaves edged silver. Female producing red fruits in the autumn. Ideal for the small garden. Height 4.5m. Spread 3m (15ft x 10ft).

Juniperus chinensis aurea -
(Fastigiate- ie, straight, columnar, tapering to a point) Young's golden juniper is very slow growing but will eventually become a columnar cone shaped tree. Foliage is pale green and yellow. No flowers and no fruits. Needs light shade to avoid summer leaf scorch. Height 4m. Spread 1m (13ft x 3ft).

Prunus lusitanica -
The Portugal laurel. This is a very attractive round headed tree. Dark glossy green leaves and in summer it carries spikes of white fragrant flowers followed by dark red fruits in autumn. Good in any situation. Height 4.5m. spread 3m (15ft x 10ft).

Salix caprea pendula -
The Kilmarnock willow has weeping branches which carry pussy willow catkins in spring. It is also known as 'weeping sally' and 'the pussy willow'. Needs well drained fertile soil and full sun. Height when well grown is 2m. Spread 1.2m. (6.6ins x 4ft.)

Sorbus Vilmorinii -
This is a particularly graceful and attractive tree. The fern like leaves are semi-weeping. Masses of pink berries appear in autumn. Makes an ideal specimen tree. It is deciduous. Height 3m and spread 3m (10ft x 10ft).

Taxus baccata fastigiata -
The Irish yew is a slender straight growing tree with small dark green foliage. Growth is very slow. Height eventually 4.5m and spread 1m (15ft x 3ft).

Laburnum vosii

Chamaecyparis Pisifera - a conical conifer with horizontal branches.